AF375424

Published by Cypress Hills Press Brooklyn, New York

Book design: Richard Tackett
http://www.richtackett.com

EDWARD VII: THE SERIES

BY
SCOTT PALMER

INTRODUCTION

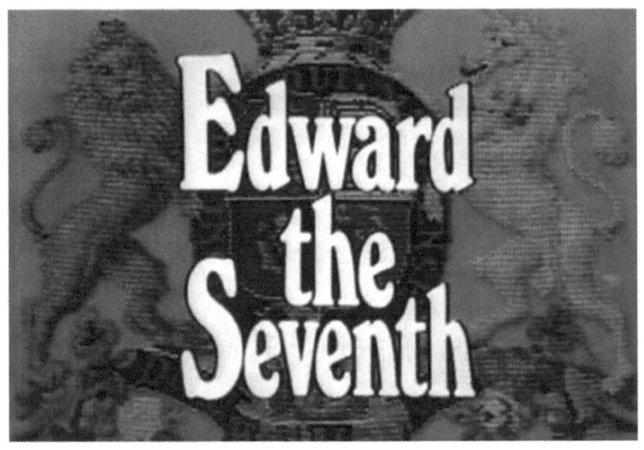

This is a reference book on the 1975 TV serial *Edward VII*, starring Timothy West and Annette Crosbie. The book includes all episodes in original date order, complete cast list, numerous photographs, directorial credits, and a story synopsis for each episode.

Based on the 1964 biography of King Edward VII by Philip Magnus, it starred Annette Crosbie as Queen Victoria, Timothy West as the elder Edward VII, and Helen Ryan as the elder Queen Alexandra.

It was directed by John Gorrie, who also wrote several episodes. David Butler wrote the majority of the series. The £2 million, 13-part biopic from ATV was a major triumph for ITV.

It was first broadcast between April and July 1975. The series looked closely at the life and loves of the Prince and also focused on the personality of the great Queen herself and other members of the royal family.

With scenes filmed within Osborne House, Sandringham, and St. George's Chapel at Windsor Castle, the series was much applauded for its attention to detail, production techniques and the performances of the lead actors.

Annette Crosbie won BAFTA's best actress award for her portrayal of Queen Victoria from a young girl to the aged, disgruntled Queen. The series ended with around 16 million viewers as #1 in the ratings. Five of the 13 episodes had also hit the top spot.

The series is about Albert Edward, known as Bertie to family and friends, the Prince of Wales (for almost sixty years) and then King Edward VII of the British Empire from 1901-1910.

It spans his entire life, from his birth in 1841, his childhood under the stern upbringing by Victoria and her husband Prince Albert, his adult lifestyle, and his ascension to the throne, to his death in 1910.

TABLE OF CONTENTS:

THE BOY EPISODE 1

DIRECTED BY John Gorrie
ORIGINAL AIR DATE: 4/1/75

CAST

Annette Crosbie..........Queen Victoria
Robert Hardy.................Prince Albert
Patience Collier........Baroness Lehzen
Alison Leggatt..........Duchess of Kent
Joseph O'Conor..Viscount Melbourne
Noel Willman......Baron Christian Von Stockmar
John Welsh..........Duke of Wellington
Michael Barrington..........Robert Peel
Moultrie Kelsall.........Sir James Clark
Peggy Ann Wood.........Lady Lyttleton
Hilary Mason.................Mrs. Roberts
Patricia Hamilton..............Mrs. Lilley
Tom Criddle....Archbishop of Canterbury
Trevor Baxter.........Bishop of London
Lee Fox............Frederick Wilhelm IV
James Warwick..............Prince Ernest
Nigel Crewe..........Lord Alfred Paget
Michael Elder.............................Grant
Katherine Hensler......................Pussy
Carl Hughes.................................Boy
Walter Henry..............Palace Official

Annette Crosbie

Robert Hardy

Patience Collier

Alison Leggatt

Joseph O'Conor

Noel Willman

John Welsh

Michael Barrington

Moultrie Kelsall   Peggy Ann Wood   Hilary Mason   Patricia Hamilton   Tom Criddle   Trevor Baxter

Lee Fox   James Warwick   Nigel Crewe   Katherine Hensler   Carl Hughes   Walter Henry

Royal Infant 1   Royal Infant 2

After only a year of marriage, Queen Victoria has not only given birth to a daughter but learns that she is again pregnant. The Queen takes her role seriously and is fully engaged in matters of State.

Noel Willman, Joseph O'Conor, John Welsh

Robert Hardy with the baby

She has an outstanding relationship with the Prime Minister, Lord Melbourne and is concerned that her confinement will limit her abilities to rule.

Prince Albert's minimal role in the household causes friction in the royal marriage. He has no say in the hiring of the household staff or the way his child is cared for.

After playing with his infant daughter, her minder, Mrs. Roberts appears. When Albert says it may be time to change the baby, she tells him that instructions for the nursery are given by Baroness Lehzen.

Noel Willman, Robert Hardy

Alison Leggatt and friend

Noel Willman, Walter Henry, Trevor Baxter, John Welsh

Baron Von Stockmar tells Albert that he must tread carefully, while Albert's brother Ernest tells him to put his foot down before it becomes too late.

More importantly Albert yearns for a role as an adviser in the political realm. The Queen dearly loves him and over time, he slowly establishes himself as the head of the household and becomes an indispensable adviser.

Robert Hardy, Infant, Hilary Mason

Joseph O'Conor, Robert Hardy, Noel Willman

Patricia Hamilton, Patience Collier

The birth of their second child, Prince Albert Edward, provides the line with a male heir. Even though he's only still a baby, his father is already planning his education.

When the royal daughter comes down with a fever, Albert is appalled to learn that she has been kept on chicken broth and milk for two weeks. Baroness Lehzen comes under criticism, and decides to leave.

When she gets well, Albert turns his attention to his son; he wants the most eminent men in the country to come up with a system for the child's education. His character must be developed using strict discipline.

Noel Willman, Robert Hardy

Robert Hardy, Annette Crosbie

AN EXPERIMENT IN EDUCATION EPISODE 2

DIRECTED BY John Gorrie
ORIGINAL AIR DATE: 4/8/75

CAST

Annette Crosbie..........Queen Victoria
Robert Hardy...................Prince Albert
Alison Leggatt..........Duchess of Kent
Felicity Kendal............Princess Vicky
Andre Morell............Lord Palmerston
Harry Andrews..............Colonel Bruce
Noel Willman...Baron Christian Von Stockmar
Charles Sturridge.......................Bertie
Simon Gipps-Kent......Younger Bertie
Terrence Hardiman............F.W. Gibbs
Arthur Hewlett.........Earl of Aberdeen
Michael Byrne.............................Fritz
Julian Sherrier.................Napoleon III
Chloe Ashcroft........Empress Eugenie
Ian Gelder.....................................Alfie
Stephen Grover.............Younger Alfie
Peter Spraggon.............Drill Sergeant
Bill Ward................................Gardener
Malcolm Rogers.......Reverend Tarver
Mandy Tulloch...........................Alice
Patricia O'Brian.......................Helena

Annette Crosbie

Robert Hardy

Alison Leggatt

Felicity Kendal

Andre Morell

Harry Andrews

Noel Willman

Charles Sturridge

Lisa Welsford..............................Louise
Oliver Rudolf.................Arthur Age 6
Paul O'Connor...............Arthur Age 3
Joshua Bassett.............Leopold Age 3
Timothy Lines......Charles Carrington
David Arnold, Roger Eden, Barnaby
Shaw.....................................Eton Boys

Simon Gipps-Kent   Terrence Hardiman

Arthur Hewlett   Michael Byrne

Julian Sherrier   Chloe Ashcroft   Ian Gelder   Stephen Grover   Peter Spraggon   Bill Ward

Lisa Welsford   Timothy Lines

The young Prince Albert, called Bertie by members of the family, is not having a happy childhood. His father has very definite ideas about his son's education, including the need for non-stop work, both in the classroom and out, and very strict discipline.

Bertie rebels but the only solution seems to be even more discipline. He is clearly a disappointment to his father who had hoped his son would be a new kind of leader.

He was hoping that his son would be a scholar who knows and understands the world but that is clearly not to be, at least not to Albert's satisfaction.

Annette Crosbie, Robert Hardy

Michael Byrne, Felicity Kendal

Robert Hardy, Annette Crosbie

He soon dismisses his eldest son and spends most of his time ensuring the happiness of his eldest daughter Princess Victoria, known as Vicky. Her marriage is something of a sad time for the Queen and the Prince Consort.

They miss her greatly and Bertie feels that he cannot replace his sister in their hearts. Bertie for his part wants to do something useful but his personal wants and desires seem to the furthest thing from his father's mind.

Annette Crosbie, Alison Leggatt, Arthur Hewlett

Terrence Hardiman, Robert Hardy

When tutor Gibbs suggests that Bertie should associate with other boys, Baron Von Stockmar agrees, but Prince Albert says the answer to the problem is more and harsher discipline.

Annette Crosbie at the ball

Robert Hardy, Noel Willman, Annette Crosbie

Robert Hardy, Noel Willman

Annette Crosbie, Simon Gipps-Kent

Several years go by, and Bertie seems to be getting nowhere with his studies. Meanwhile, after serving Prince Albert for over 20 years, Count Von Stockmar says he is getting old, and will return to Coburg.

After Vicky's wedding, Prince Albert says that Bertie is now their eldest child, and should be given a certain degree of freedom, and a share in their work, as Albert puts it.

He tells Bertie that Colonel Bruce, a distinguished officer from the Grenadier Guards, will be put in charge of Bertie to teach him what will be expected from him in life.

Robert Hardy, Felicity Kendal

THE NEW WORLD EPISODE 3

DIRECTED BY John Gorrie
ORIGINAL AIR DATE: 4/15/75

CAST

Annette Crosbie..........Queen Victoria
Robert Hardy..................Prince Albert
Alison Leggatt..........Duchess of Kent
Felicity Kendal............Princess Vicky
Andre Morell...........Lord Palmerston
Harry Andrews..............Colonel Bruce
Charles Sturridge......................Bertie
Michael Byrne...........................Fritz
Guy Slater.............Charles Carrington
Nigel Havers.........Frederick Crichton
Virginia Clarke.............Nellie Clifden
David Freedman......Natty Rothschild
George Belbin..........Sir George Brown
Peter Cartwright............Colonel Percy
Glenn Williams..........Sergeant Major
Michael Elder.............................Grant
Peter Carlisle......President Buchanan
Christopher Malcolm...American Attache
Nan Munro..................Mrs. Schuyler
Elliott Sullivan.....................Prisoner
David Lander...........Prison Governor

Annette Crosbie   Robert Hardy

Alison Leggatt   Felicity Kendal

Andre Morell   Harry Andrews

Charles Sturridge   Michael Byrne

Shirley Steedman........................Alice
Ian Gelder.................................Alfie
Deborah Makepeace...............Helena
Philippa Robinson..................Louise
Paul Sutch...............................Arthur
Ian Sutch................................Leopold
Fanny Bassett........................Beatrice
Nicholas Lane...........................Willy
Billy Miller............................Violinist
Kathryn Leigh Scott....Buchanan's Niece

Guy Slater   Nigel Havers

Virginia Clarke   David Freedman

George Belbin   Peter Cartwright   Glenn Williams   Peter Carlisle   Christopher Malcolm   Nan Munro

Elliott Sullivan   David Lander   Shirley Steedman   Ian Gelder   Deborah Makepeace   Kathryn Leigh Scott

Guard

After a successful tour of America, young Prince Bertie returns home to find that his parents do not see it as a personal success, rather one that can be attributed to the monarchy in general.

However, it was Bertie who was the success; whether meeting President Buchanan and his niece, planting a small tree near the grave of George Washington, or charming people at a ball.

Alison Leggatt with the baby

Charles Sturridge, Harry Andrews, Christopher Malcolm,
David Lander, Guard

Christopher Malcolm, Harry Andrews

His father tells him he is to go to Oxford to continue his studies but will be under the care of a governor and will not be
allowed to mix with other students.

Prime Minister Lord Palmerston tells Prince Albert that perhaps Bertie should take more of an active part in some purely ceremonial duties, but Albert says he will not expose him to society as yet.

Charles Sturridge, Harry Andrews. Christopher Malcolm

Annette Crosbie, Robert Hardy

Lord Palmerston brings news that in America, the Southern states have seceded from the Union, and the question now is does England consider them rebels, or recognize them as a new nation?

Andre Morell, Robert Hardy

Annette Crosbie, Robert Hardy

Annette Crosbie, Alison Leggatt

Annette Crosbie, Robert Hardy

Bertie really wants to join the army but his father refuses, eventually deciding in his favor. He is made a Lieutenant Colonel in the Grenadier Guards and sent to Ireland to undergo his training.

Colonel Percy tells Colonel Bruce-who is still on hand to monitor Bertie's activities-that the young Prince is different than he expected. Bruce says that Bertie is very willing to learn.

There he sees a few familiar faces, including Charles Carrington, and begins an affair with an Irish music hall performer and singer named Nellie Clifden.

Michael Byrne, Robert Hardy

ALIX EPISODE 4

DIRECTED BY John Gorrie
ORIGINAL AIR DATE: 4/22/75

CAST

Annette Crosbie..........Queen Victoria
Robert Hardy.................Prince Albert
Felicity Kendal.............Princess Vicky
Andre Morell............Lord Palmerston
Harry Andrews.............General Bruce
Charles Sturridge......................Bertie
Deborah Grant......Princess Alexandra
Anthony Douse.........Prince Christian
Kathleen Byron......Princess Christian
Gwyneth Strong.....................Minny
Shirley Steedman......................Alice
Ian Gelder......................................Alfie
Deborah Makepeace................Helena
Susan Macready................Wally Paget
Peter Penry-Jones.......Augustus Paget
Michael Byrne.............................Fritz
Guy Slater.............Charles Carrington
Nigel Havers.........Frederick Crichton
Peter Collingwood....Lord John Russell
Moultrie Kelsall....................Dr. Clark
Jeffrey Segal......................Dr. Jenner

Annette Crosbie   Robert Hardy

Felicity Kendal   Andre Morell

Harry Andrews   Charles Sturridge

Deborah Grant   Anthony Douse

Ralph Watson....................Dr. Watson
John Dunbar...............Dean Wellesley
Max Hartnell........................Equerry

Kathleen Byron

Gwyneth Strong

Shirley Steedman

Ian Gelder

Susan Macready

Peter Penry-Jones

Michael Byrne

Guy Slater

Nigel Havers

Peter Collingwood

Moultrie Kelsall

Jeffrey Segal

Ralph Watson

John Dunbar

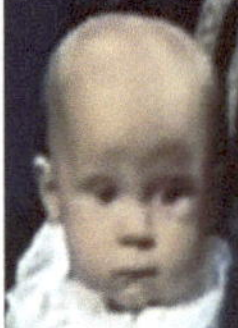
Max Hartnell

Marie

Vicky's Baby

Prince Bertie continues his military training, but he is taken to deceiving his superiors and sneaking off with his friends to the music halls. His parents continue their search to find Bertie a suitable wife.

Wally Paget travels to Denmark, where she meets Princess Alexandra. She doesn't give the real reason for her visit, but later tells Vicky she was very impressed with the Princess.

Bertie's parents' preference is for a German bride but eventually settle on Princess Alexandra of Denmark, known to her friends as Alix. A brief meeting is arranged for the two to meet but no final decision is made.

Susan Macready, Kathleen Byron

Robert Hardy, Harry Andrews

Deborah Grant, Kathleen Byron

Alix's father, Prince Christian, tells his daughter that some-day Bertie will be King of England. Whoever marries him will becomes the queen of the greatest empire the world has ever known.

But Bertie's response to Princess Alexandra is less than en-
thusiastic, leading to an argument between Queen Victoria
and Prince Albert. The Prince says his son certainly does
not look like a young man in love.

Robert Hardy, Annette Crosbie

Harry Andrews, Charles Sturridge

But Albert tells Bertie that he must marry Alexandra; the marriage would be important to the country, morally, social-ly, and politically. He gives Bertie six weeks-until the end of the year-to decide.

Susan Macready, Andre Morell

Robert Hardy, Annette Crosbie

Robert Hardy, Jeffrey Segal, Moultrie Kelsall

Relations with his father deteriorate even further when the Prince Consort receives a confidential letter from Von Stockmar telling of Bertie's dalliance with a music hall singer.

At the end of 1861, Prince Albert becomes ill and doctors are sent for. Victoria tells the children that their father is suffering from a chill and overwork. Unfortunately, the Prince has typhoid-which soon kills him.

Felicity Kendal, Susan Macready

Annette Crosbie, Susan Macready

A HUNDRED THOUSAND WELCOMES
EPISODE 5

DIRECTED BY John Gorrie
ORIGINAL AIR DATE: 4/29/75

CAST

Annette Crosbie..........Queen Victoria
Timothy West.............................Bertie
Felicity Kendal............Princess Vicky
Deborah Grant......Princess Alexandra
Michael Hordern........W.E. Gladstone
Andre Morell............Lord Palmerston
Kathleen Byron......Princess Christian
Anthony Douse.........Prince Christian
Gwyneth Strong.......................Minny
Michael Byrne............................Fritz
Susan Macready...............Wally Paget
Shirley Steedman........................Alice
Ian Gelder..................................Alfie
Deborah Makepeace...............Helena
Phillipa Robinson....................Louise
John Boswall...............King Leopold
Peter Collingwood....Lord John Russell
Edward Jewesbury......Lord Granville
Rhoda Lewis..........Lady Macclesfield
Paul Greenhalgh..........Prince William
Emma Neal..........................Beatrice

Annette Crosbie   Timothy West

Felicity Kendal   Deborah Grant

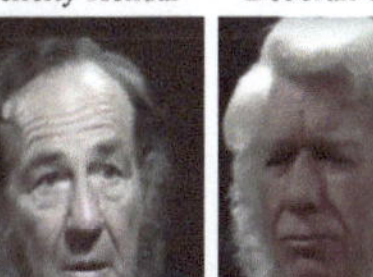

Michael Hordern   Andre Morell

Kathleen Byron   Anthony Douse

Donald Bisset....................Dr. Brown
Reginald Barratt.......................Mayor
Max Hartnell.......................Equerry
Alison Crook..............Princess Thyra
Anthony Hambleton...Prince Leopold
Peter Richards...............Prince Arthur
Christine Blair..........Lady in Waiting
John Smart...............Cabinet Minister

Gwyneth Strong   Michael Byrne

Susan Macready   Shirley Steedman

Ian Gelder   Deborah Makepeace   John Boswall   Peter Collingwood   Edward Jewesbury   Rhoda Lewis

Paul Greenhalgh   Emma Neal   Donald Bisset   Reginald Barratt   Max Hartnell   Anthony Hambleton

Peter Richards   John Smart   Guest 1

Prince Albert is laid to rest. With Queen Victoria deep in mourning, the Cabinet is concerned that her withdrawal from public duties will have a negative impact on her people.

With his mother deeply in grief, Bertie assumes many of the public duties of the monarch. He proves to be quite popular and works hard at maintaining the positive face of the monarchy.

It's not quite what Bertie had in mind, but the Queen refuses any role for him in matters of State. She sees him as an utter failure and refuses to let him participate in any decision-making.

Annette Crosbie, Timothy West

Queen Victoria meanwhile travels to meet Prince and Princess Christian, the parents of Alexandra. When she and Bertie get together, they both warm to each other. Victoria says the wedding will take place in March.

Deborah Makepeace, Shirley Steedman

Queen Victoria in mourning

Prince Albert lies in state

Deborah Grant, Timothy West

The Queen also decides that there is no need to wait the full year of mourning before Bertie can marry and she pushes him to decide on Alix. He and Princess Alix are married and she soon after announces that she is pregnant.

Lord Palmerston says tells Bertie that the Queen is in a di-lemma; more often than not, her ministers were seen by Prince Albert, so she will have to learn how to govern.

Felicity Kendal, Timothy West, Michael Byrne

Michael Hordern, Peter Collingwood, Andre Morell

Edward Jewesbury, Michael Hordern

Timothy West, Andre Morell

But Bertie tells Palmerston that he is married, over 21, and the heir to the throne, so he feels he should do something for his country. Palmerston agrees. Now all they have to do is convince Victoria.

Timothy West, Deborah Grant

When she won't budge, Palmerston gives Bertie things to do; when Victoria finds out, she is angry. She considers Bertie having amusements in society, and says only she, the sovereign, can represent the monarchy in public.

Soon, Alix gives birth to a son-after only seven months of pregnancy. Although it only weighs three pounds, Dr. Brown tells Bertie that mother and baby are both doing fine.

THE INVISIBLE QUEEN EPISODE 6

DIRECTED BY John Gorrie
ORIGINAL AIR DATE: 5/6/75

CAST

Annette Crosbie..........Queen Victoria
Timothy West...........................Bertie
Helen Ryan...........Princess Alexandra
John Gielgud..........Benjamin Disraeli
Michael Hordern........W.E. Gladstone
Jane Lapotaire..........Princess Dagmar
Guy Slater.............Charles Carrington
Bruce Purchase......Czarevitch Alexander
Kathleen Byron..Queen Louise of Denmark
Paul Greenhalgh...George I of Greece
William Dysart...............John Brown
Bryan Coleman.............Earl of Derby
Shirley Steedman.......................Alice
Deborah Makepeace...............Helena
Ian Gelder...................................Alfie
Rhoda Lewis..........Lady Macclesfield
Michael Gwilym...Sir Charles Mordant
Geoffrey Wincott...King Wilhelm I of Prussia
Edgar Wreford....Sir William Knollys
Ivor Roberts.............Dr. William Gull
Rula Lenska.........Hortense Schneider

Annette Crosbie

Timothy West

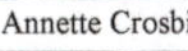

Helen Ryan

John Gielgud

Michael Hordern

Jane Lapotaire

Guy Slater

Bruce Purchase

Jonathan Adams..........Sgt. Ballantyne
Anna Wing................Countrywoman
Ludmilla Nova..........Lady Mordaunt
Samuel West........Albert Victor Age 5
Joseph West............................George
Heidi Elphick...........................Louise

Kathleen Byron

Paul Greenhalgh

William Dysart

Bryan Coleman

Shirley Steedman

Deborah Makepeac

Ian Gelder

Michael Gwilym

Geoffrey Wincott

Edgar Wreford

Ivor Roberts

Rula Lenska

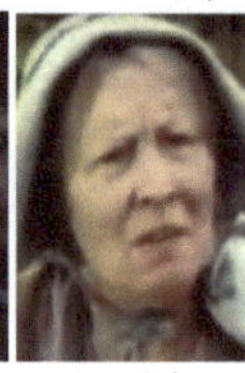

Jonathan Adams

Anna Wing

Joseph West

Heidi Elphick

Bertie's family continues to grow but Princess Alix is not strong and suffers from general ill health. She is concerned that Bertie's sister Helena is being forced into a marriage with a man much older than se is.

Before Alix gives birth to another child, Dr. William Gull tells Bertie that the rheumatic fever in her thighs and hips has grown worse. She will not lose the baby, but once again it will be premature.

When Benjamin Disraeli congratulates Victoria on the birth of another grandchild, she tells him that once again, she missed the birth. She blames their "self-indulgent way of life" for Alix's weak health.

Edgar Wreford, Ivor Roberts

Politics continue to cause a rift in the family with Princess Alix refusing to see or have anything to do with Bertie's German relations after the forced annexation of parts of Denmark.

John Gielgud, Annette Crosbie

John Gielgud, Bryan Coleman

John Gielgud, Annette Crosbie

Timothy West, John Gielgud

It all comes to a head when the King of Prussia asks to call on her. Queen Victoria continues to refuse all public engagements and there is a rise in Republicanism.

Alix decides, against her will, to receive the King of Prussia.
Bertie thanks her for doing it, and says that his mother will
be pleased. Alix says she did not do it for Victoria-or even
England. She did it for Bertie.

Timothy West, Helen Ryan

Helen Ryan, Paul Greenhalgh

Paul Greenhalgh, Jane Lapotaire, Bruce Purchase

Ian Gelder, Edgar Wreford

Bertie finds himself in court as a witness in a divorce case involving a lady with whom he had a dalliance. The divorce petition fails when Lady Mordaunt is found to be insane.

Prime Minister Gladstone tries to have the Queen appoint Bertie as Viceroy of Ireland but she rejects the suggestion. She is adamant in her refusal.

Everyone expects the worst when Bertie contracts typhoid and approaches death on the 10th anniversary of his father dying from the same disease. Miraculously however, he recovers.

Timothy West, Edgar Wreford

DEAREST PRINCE EPISODE 7

DIRECTED BY John Gorrie
ORIGINAL AIR DATE: 5/13/75

CAST

Annette Crosbie..........Queen Victoria
Timothy West..............................Bertie
Helen Ryan...........Princess Alexandra
John Gielgud..........Benjamin Disraeli
Jane Lapotaire..........Princess Dagmar
Francesca Annis............Lillie Langtry
Guy Slater....Lord Charles Carrington
Bruce Purchase......Czarevitch Alexander
Joyce Carey............Lady Chesterfield
Gareth Thomas...........Lord Beresford
Robert Mill..................Lord Blandford
Derek Fowlds...Lord Randolph Churchill
Jeffry Wickham..........Lord Aylesford
Teresa White...............Lady Aylesford
Peter Howell..............Francis Knollys
Barbara Laurenson....Charlotte Knollys
Anthony Dawes............Lord Alington
John Normington.......Oliver Montagu
William Dysart...............John Brown
William Abney..........Sir Allen Young
Trevor Peacock.......George Leyboune

Annette Crosbie

Timothy West

Helen Ryan

John Gielgud

Jane Lapotaire

Francesca Annis

Guy Slater

Bruce Purchase

Jerome Watts...................Prince Eddy
Christopher Watts.........Prince George
Vanessa Vane..............Princess Louise
Samantha Gates........Princess Victoria
Monique Kaufman.......Princess Maud
Dickon Paine..............Prince Nicholas
Eric Hillyard.............Cabinet Minister
Anthony Woodruff..Cabinet Secretary
Mischa De La Motte...Williams-Footman

Joyce Carey

Gareth Thomas

Robert Mill

Derek Fowlds

Jeffry Wickham

Teresa White.

Peter Howell

Barbara Laurenson

Anthony Dawes

John Normington

William Dysart

William Abney

Trevor Peacock

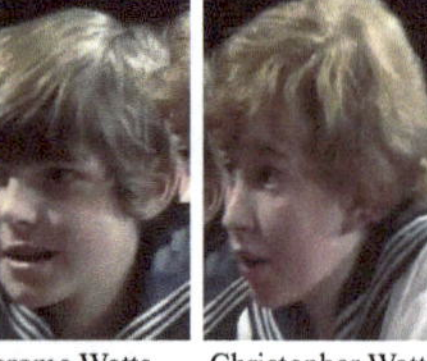

Jerome Watts

Christopher Watts

Vanessa Vane

Anthony Woodruff

Mischa De La Motte

The Queen continues to refuse all attempts at giving her eldest son any responsibility in matters of State. This is a constant state of frustration for Bertie.

After a very successful visit to Coventry, the new Prime Minister, Mr. Disraeli, looks for something appropriate for the Prince to do. Bertie suggests that he go on an official State visit to India.

To Bertie's surprise and delight, Victoria agrees. It causes major difficulties at home when he informs Alix that she will not be accompanying him. It had always been her dream to visit India and is heartbroken at being left behind.

Annette Crosbie, Helen Ryan

Gareth Thomas, Timothy West

Robert Mill, John Gielgud

John Gielgud, Derek Fowlds

The trip to India goes well but Bertie must face yet another scandal when Lord Aylesford announces that his wife has been having an affair and he may be divorcing her.

Lord Randolph Churchill offers to intervene in the case - the other party in the tryst is his brother - if the Prince would also intervene with Lord Aylesford to stop a divorce. Bertie flatly refuses, leaving Churchill to try to force the Prince's hand.

TV Poster

Francis Knollys tells Bertie that a divorce would ruin both families involved, but the Prince says that he cannot interfere in a private matter; if people can't manage their affairs more sensibly, they don't deserve to have them.

John Gielgud, Joyce Carey

John Gielgud, Timothy West

Timothy West, Jeffrey Wickham

Derek Fowlds, Anthony Dawes

Later, after being ignored, Lord Randolph pays a visit to Alix, along with Lord Alington and Lady Aylesford. He says he has letters from Bertie in his possession which were written to Lady Aylesford.

Alix is outraged, and tells them to leave. She later tells the Queen and Disraeli. When Bertie hears about the blackmail, he challengers Lord Randolph to a duel-with pistols.

Of course that does not happen, and the situation is resolved. A few days later at a ball, Sir Allen Young introduces the Prince to Lillie-Mrs. Edward Langtry.

Bertie has a cup of tea

THE ROYAL QUADRILLE EPISODE 8

DIRECTED BY John Gorrie
ORIGINAL AIR DATE: 5/20/75

CAST

Annette Crosbie..........Queen Victoria
Timothy West.............Prince of Wales
Helen Ryan...........Princess Alexandra
Michael Hordern........W.E. Gladstone
Felicity Kendal............Princess Vicky
Jane Lapotaire.........Empress Dagmar
Christopher Neame....Prince Wilhelm
Francesca Annis............Lillie Langtry
Brewster Mason...................Bismarck
Michael Byrne...........................Fritz
Bruce Purchase.....Czar Alexander III
Paul Greenhalgh...George I of Greece
John Normington.......Oliver Montagu
Richard Leech..........Sir George Dilke
Guy Slater................Lord Carrington
William Dysart...............John Brown
Charles Dance...............Prince Eddy
Michael Osborne..........Prince George
Zibba Mays.................Mrs. Crawford
Cheryl Campbell.....Princess Beatrice
Vanessa Miles...........Princess Louise

Annette Crosbie

Timothy West

Helen Ryan

Michael Hordern

Felicity Kendal

Jane Lapotaire

Christopher Neame

Francesca Annis

Madeleine Cannon........Princess Toria
Rosalyn Elvin...............Princess Maud
Barbara Laurenson.......Charlotte Knollys
Dan Meaden................Danish Farmer
Basil Clarke..................Dr. Buchanan
David Purcell....................................P.C.
Edwin Brown..........................Cabbie
Victor Harrington, Anthony Lang.......
....Lords

Brewster Mason

Michael Byrne

Bruce Purchase

Paul Greenhalgh

John Normington

Richard Leech

Guy Slater

William Dysart

Charles Dance

Michael Osborne

Zibba Mays

Cheryl Campbell

Dan Meaden

Basil Clarke

Diner

Maitre D

1882-1888: Bertie visits Denmark along with the Russian Czar and the King of Greece. He also visits his sister Vicky and her husband Fritz, the Crown Prince of Prussia.

Vicky is concerned about her son William whom she knows will some day be Emperor and has fallen under the spell of Bismarck, who they dislike with a passion.

When the British intervene to put down a mutiny in the Egyptian army, Bertie wants to go to Egypt with the Household Cavalry, but Victoria says it is out of the question.

64

The Queen also states that she is an old lady and tires very easily these days; Bertie may be "called upon at any moment." Gladstone tells the Queen that Bertie does not believe her.

Helen Ryan, Annette Crosbie

Felicity Kendal, Michael Byrne

Timothy West as the Prince of Wales

Bertie continues his liaison with Lillie Langtry, which takes the sting out of not being allowed to go to Egypt. When she gets a bad review for her latest play, Gladstone tells her to ignore the critics. Alix agrees.

Prime Minister Gladstone asks the Prince to serve on a Royal Commission on the state of housing for the working classes. Lord Carrington has agreed to serve with the Prince.

Jane Lapotaire, Helen Ryan

Helen Ryan, Felicity Kendal

Annette Crosbie, Timothy West

Guy Slater, Timothy West

Bertie tours some of the poorest districts and is appalled at the conditions he finds there. He and Lord Carrington go to the area in disguise.

Guy Slater, Timothy West

Michael Osborne, Charles Dance

Michael Hordern as W.E. Gladstone

When he gets back from the trip, he heads to the House of Lords, where he makes an impassioned speech for better housing conditions. Meanwhile, the Queen is mourning the death of the faithful John Brown.

SCANDAL EPISODE 9

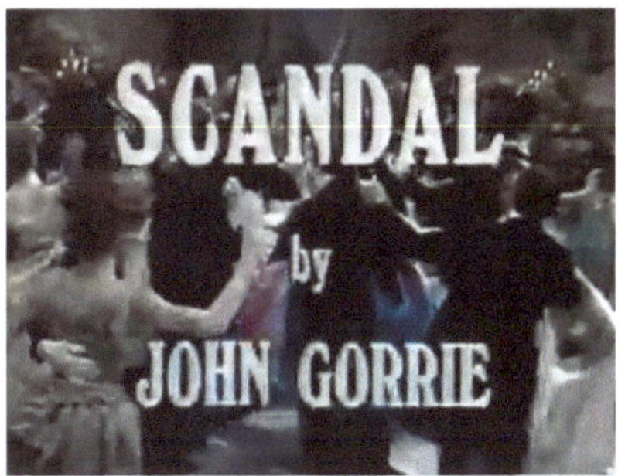

DIRECTED BY John Gorrie
ORIGINAL AIR DATE: 5/27/75

CAST

Annette Crosbie..........Queen Victoria
Timothy West...........................Bertie
Helen Ryan...........Princess Alexandra
Michael Hordern........W.E. Gladstone
Richard Vernon..........Lord Salisbury
Robert Flemyng...........Lord Coventry
Carolyn Seymour...........Lady Brooke
Peter Howell..............Francis Knollys
John Normington.......Oliver Montagu
Edward Hardwicke......Lord Rosebery
Charles Dance.................Prince Eddy
Michael Osborne..........Prince George
Clive Morton....Lt. General Owen Williams
Donald Douglas..Sir William Gordon Cumming
Gareth Thomas...Lord Charles Beresford
Nancie Jackson..........Lady Beresford
John Carlin..................George Lewis
Frederick Treves....Christopher Sykes
John Harding.............Berkeley Levett
Terence Wilton...............Lycett Green
John Byron...................Arthur Wilson

Annette Crosbie

Timothy West

Helen Ryan

Michael Hordern

Richard Vernon

Robert Flemyng

Carolyn Seymour

Peter Howell

Graham Seed...........Arthur Wilson Jr.
Margot Van Der Burgh.....Mrs. Arthur Wilson
Geoffrey Palmer....Sir Edward Clarke
Vanessa Miles............Princess Louise
Madeleine Cannon........Princess Toria
Rosalyn Elvin..............Princess Maud
Judy Loe........................Princess May
Mel Churcher.............Princess Helene
Ronald Mayer................Village Priest

John Normington

Edward Hardwicke

Charles Dance

Michael Osborne

Clive Morton

Donald Douglas

Gareth Thomas

Nancie Jackson

John Carlin

Frederick Treves

John Harding

Terence Wilton

John Byron

Graham Seed

Margot Van Der Burgh

Geoffrey Palmer

Vanessa Miles

Madeleine Cannon

Rosalyn Elvin

Judy Loe

Mel Churcher

Guest

Mrs. Green

1890-1893: Bertie faces scandal on several fronts. He agrees to assist Lady Brooke to retrieve a letter she wrote to her one-time lover, Lord Charles Beresford.

Violinists playing

Richard Vernon, Annette Crosbie

She is now terrified that Lady Beresford will take some action against her. When Alix sees Bertie take Lady Brooke aside, she wrongly assumes it is a romantic assignation.

Clive Morton, Robert Flemyng

Carolyn Seymour, Gareth Thomas

Timothy West, Gareth Thomas

Bertie calls on George Lewis, Lady Beresford's lawyer and orders him to destroy the letter. Lewis tells him that it is not his to destroy. However, he will suggest to Lady Beresford that she destroy it.

Lewis says that he cannot guarantee that Lady Beresford will take his advice, but the Prince says at least he can tell Lady Brooke that every effort is being made.

John Normington, Helen Ryan

Robert Flemyng, Clive Morton

Timothy West, Clive Morton, Robert Flemyng

Geoffrey Palmer in court

When Charles Beresford hears of the Prince's action, he confronts Bertie and demands an apology with the threat of making the whole thing public.

A second scandal erupts when Lieutenant Colonel Sir William Gordon Cumming is found cheating at cards. He was seen cheating by five different people.

The Prince and others try to settle the matter quietly by having Cumming sign a paper, but Cumming sues to regain his good name and reputation and it all becomes public.

Alix and Bertie encourage their eldest son, Prince Eddy, to find a suitable young woman and marry. Although he does eventually find someone, he falls ill and dies.

Carolyn Seymour, Timothy West

THE YEARS OF WAITING EPISODE 10

DIRECTED BY John Gorrie
ORIGINAL AIR DATE: 6/3/75

CAST

Annette Crosbie..........Queen Victoria
Timothy West..........................Bertie
Helen Ryan...........Princess Alexandra
Michael Hordern........W.E. Gladstone
Felicity Kendal............Princess Vicky
Jane Lapotaire...Dowager Empress Dagmar
Christopher Neame...Kaiser Wilhelm II
Richard Vernon...........Lord Salisbury
Moira Redmond.............Alice Keppel
Carolyn Seymour....Lady Daisy Warwick
Lyndon Brook...................A.J. Balfour
Edward Hardwicke......Lord Rosebery
Peter Howell..............Francis Knollys
Barbara Laurenson....Charlotte Knollys
Michael Osborne..........Prince George
Judy Loe.......................Princess May
Sally Home..................Agnes Keyser
Cheryl Campbell.....Princess Beatrice
Vanessa Miles............Princess Louise
Madeleine Cannon.......Princess Toria
Rosalyn Elvin..............Princess Maud

Annette Crosbie

Timothy West

Helen Ryan

Michael Hordern

Felicity Kendal

Jane Lapotaire

Christopher Neame

Richard Vernon

Meriel Brooke.......Czarina Alexandra
Robert Robinson............Ernest Cassel
Rosamond Burne........Mrs. Gladstone
Norman Shelley...........Sir James Reid
Dennis Chinnery.....Randall Davidson
Adrienne Posta.................Marie Lloyd
Michael Billington....Czar Nicholas II
Edward Brooks..........Alberta Captain
Martin Skinner...........................Sipido
Victor Harrington...Peer at Westminster Abbey
Bobby Monro...............Sword Dancer
James Caution, David Milner, Bob
Murphy................................Bagpipers

Moira Redmond

Carolyn Seymour

Lyndon Brook   Edward Hardwicke

Peter Howell   Barbara Laurenson

Michael Osborne

Judy Loe

Sally Home

Cheryl Campbell

Madeleine Cannon   Meriel Brooke

Robert Robinson

Rosamond Burne

Norman Shelley

Dennis Chinnery

Adrienne Posta

Michael Billington

Edward Brooks   Martin Skinner

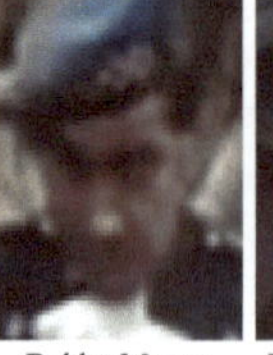

Victor Harrington

Bobby Monro   John Normington

1896-1901: Britain finds itself at war in South Africa when British colonists attack the Boer government. P.M. Salisbury tells Bertie that Cecil Rhodes sent Dr. Jameson and 400 mounted police into a raid in the Transvaal.

TV Poster

Annette Crosbie, Martin Skinner

The hope was to incite a rebellion against the Boer government of Paul Krueger. Thereby the British Dominion would stretch from Johannesburg to the cape. The raid was a failure.

But Queen Victoria still refuses to let Bertie have any role in matters of State. Bertie spends his time going to the races and as is so often the case, plays host to visiting dignitaries, this time the Czar and Czarina of Russia.

Bertie remarks to Gladstone that the country hasn't always been proud of him, to which the Prime Minister replies that the Queen is an obstinate and short-sighted old woman.

The Queen celebrates her Diamond Jubilee. She tells Alix there is to be a procession through London, stopping by the steps of St. Paul's Cathedral for a short service.

Helen Ryan, Jane Lapotaire

Peter Howell, Richard Vernon

When Gladstone dies, Bertie acts as one of the pallbearers.
Queen Victoria is upset by this; there is no precedent. When
the Queen is read an account that Bertie walked over and
kissed the hand of Mrs. Gladstone, she literally screams.

Bagpipers plat at Balmoral

Meriel Brooke, Annette Crosbie

84

Timothy West, Richard Vernon

Timothy West, Helen Ryan

Bertie is the object of an assassination attempt in Brussels while travelling on a train. He comments it was a good thing the assassin was not a very good shot.

Now quite old, Queen Victoria dies in January of 1901 and Bertie becomes King Edward the VII. When he asks the Captain of the Alberta why the flag is at half mast, he is told that the Queen is dead. "But the King lives," he replies.

Timothy West, Christopher Neame

Timothy West, Helen Ryan

KING AT LAST EPISODE 11

DIRECTED BY John Gorrie
ORIGINAL AIR DATE: 6/10/75

CAST

Timothy West..........King Edward VII
Helen Ryan..............Queen Alexandra
Richard Vernon...........Lord Salisbury
Moira Redmond.............Alice Keppel
Felicity Kendal............Princess Vicky
Michael Osborne..........Prince George
Madeleine Cannon.......Princess Toria
Judy Loe.......................Princess May
Christopher Neame......Kaiser Wilhelm II
Peter Howell..............Francis Knollys
Edward De Souza......Luis De Soveral
Lyndon Brook..................A.J. Balfour
Denis Lill............Frederick Ponsonby
Guy Slater.................Lord Carrington
Basil Hoskins...................Lord Esher
Angus MacKay........Lord Lansdowne
Kenneth Gilbert.....Sir Francis Laking
Roger Ostime.....Sir Frederick Treves
Paul Bacon........Norroy King of Arms
Roy Jacobs....................Prince David
Daniel Slater.................Prince George

Timothy West

Helen Ryan

Richard Vernon

Moira Redmond

Felicity Kendal

Michael Osborne

Madeleine Cannon

Judy Loe

Rebecca Slater..............Princess Mary
Robert Fountain, Stuart Lock...Newsboys
Keith Ashley, William Gossling, Alex
Lewis, Laon Maybanke, Mike Mungarvan, Garth Watkins, John Wilder...
....Dignitaries

Christopher Neame

Peter Howell

Edward De Souza   Lyndon Brook

Denis Lill

Guy Slater

Basil Hoskins

Angus MacKay

Kenneth Gilbert   Roger Ostime

Paul Bacon

Robert Fountain

Stuart Lock

William Gossling

Alex Lewis   Mike Mungarvan

John Wilder

Dignitary 1

Dignitary 2

Dignitary 3

Man at Coronation 1   Man at Coronation 2

Man at Proclamation 1   Man at Proclamation 2

After nearly a sixty year wait, Bertie becomes King upon the death of his mother Queen Victoria. There is some speculation as to whether he is up to the job. But he gives his ministers a rousing speech.

The King's nephew, the German Kaiser, proposes an Anglo-German alliance and the King supports it but several of his Ministers simply do not take him seriously.

The Kaiser promises to protect British interests in India and the middle East, providing England likewise promises to protect German interests in Africa and South America.

Christopher Neame, Timothy West

Although now Queen, Alix is having some trouble adjusting to their new life, refusing to live at Buckingham Palace and reluctant to leave Marlborough House, the home designated for the Prince of Wales, now their son George.

Peter Howell, Richard Vernon, Basil Hoskins

P.M. acknowledges the new King

Lyndon Brook, Richard Vernon, Angus MacKay

Peter Howell, Richard Vernon, Guy Slater, Lyndon Brook

The King's sister, Vicky - the Kaiser's mother - is dying of cancer. When Edward visits her, she warns him that her son the Kaiser is jealous, and cannot allow himself to be second to anyone-including his uncle.

Vicky sends for Ponsonby; she asks him for a service. For the past 40 years, she has had many letters from England. Some of them contain things that could be used politically against England. Ponsonby takes the letters.

Lyndon Brook, Garth Watkins, Richard Vernon, Alex Lewis, Angus MacKay, William Gossling

Helen Ryan, Peter Howell

Paul Bacon reads the proclamation

Moira Redmond, Basil Hoskins, Edward De Souza

Lord Salisbury informs the King that due to ill health, he will soon resign as prime Minister. He recommends his nephew, A.J. Balfour, to replace him.

The King is frustrated when his coronation is postponed due to the Boer War but when it is finally scheduled, it must be postponed as the King must undergo emergency surgery to remove his appendix.

Doctor Sir Francis Laking literally screams at Edward, telling him that if he does not have the operation in 24 hours, he will be dead. Sir Frederick Treves performs it, and the King pulls through.

Timothy West, Michael Osborne, Dignitary

THE PEACEMAKER EPISODE 12

DIRECTED BY John Gorrie
ORIGINAL AIR DATE: 6/17/75

CAST

Timothy West..........King Edward VII
Helen Ryan..............Queen Alexandra
Jane Lapotaire.......Dowager Empress Dagmar
Christopher Neame......Kaiser Wilhelm II
Moira Redmond.............Alice Keppel
Geoffrey Bayldon......Sir Henry Campbell-Bannerman
Lyndon Brook..................A.J. Balfour
Michael Osborne..........Prince George
Judy Loe.......................Princess May
Edward De Souza......Luis De Soveral
James Berwick............Sir John Fisher
Basil Hoskins....................Lord Esher
Guy Slater.................Lord Carrington
Angus MacKay........Lord Lansdowne
Robert Robinson......Sir Ernest Cassel
Barbara Laurenson.......Charlotte Knollys
Dennis Lill..........Frederick Ponsonby
Michael Griffiths.....Charles Hardinge
John Rutland......Sir Edmund Monson
John Scrrct...............President Loubet
Hazel McBride............Jeanne Granier

Timothy West

Helen Ryan

Jane Lapotaire

Christopher Neame

Moira Redmond

Geoffrey Bayldon

Lyndon Brook

Michael Osborne

Rosalyn Elvin..............Princess Maud
Anthony Douse............King Christian
Roy Jacobs...................Prince David
Daniel Slater................Prince George
Rebecca Slater..............Princess Mary
Arthur Quintus Haycraft......Prince Henry
Wayne Brooks..............Prince George
Michael Billington....Czar Nicholas II

Judy Loe

Edward De Souza

James Berwick

Basil Hoskins

Guy Slater

Angus MacKay

Robert Robinson

Barbara Laurenson

Dennis Lill

Michael Griffiths

John Rutland

John Serret

Hazel McBride

Rosalyn Elvin

Anthony Douse

Roy Jacobs

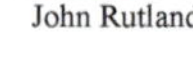

Daniel Slater

Michael Billington

Charles

Guest

The King grows increasingly irritated by his nephew the
Kaiser. He leaves a party which angers Alix. He tells her
it is not a party-it's a one-man monologue by an arrogant
booby.

His attempt at engineering a grand alliance with Germany is successful at one level but ultimately rejected by the Government who still see his His Majesty as someone not to be taken seriously.

Basil Hoskins, James Berwick, Guy Slater

Denis Lill, Timothy West

Christopher Neame, Timothy West

Helen Ryan, Timothy West

At a dinner, the King goes on about how he really thought he might be of some use; that the government would listen to his advice. It seems that important issues are decided before he even hears of them.

98

Still searching for some way to make an impact, the King announces he will soon go on a Grand Tour of several European nations including Britain's historical enemy, France.

Edward De Souza, Barbara Laurenson

Basil Hoskins, James Berwick, Robert Robinson, Moira Redmond

Prime Minister Balfour insists that the King take a representative of the government with him. Edward decides on Charles Hardinge of the Foreign Office-even though he is only an under secretary.

His arrival in France is marked by boos and catcalls, but he soon charms them and leaves to great cheers. He makes a great speech calling for an Entente Cordiale.

Lyndon Brook, Angus MacKay

Angus MacKay, Lyndon Brook

Timothy West, Geoffrey Bayldon

His nephew Willie, the German Emperor, continues to visit but has become pompous to the point that the King can barely stand being in the same room with him.

After the failure of the Grand Alliance, Germany begins to expand its army and navy. Sir John Fisher tells the King that a plan might be to smash the German Navy at its base.

Edward thinks that would be barbarous. There is one other way: since the government won't give any more money to the Navy, they must make more efficient use with what they have. Naval command must be reorganized, with an efficient reserve fleet.

Basil Hoskins, Moira Redmond

GOOD OLD TEDDY! EPISODE 13

DIRECTED BY John Gorrie
ORIGINAL AIR DATE: 7/1/75

CAST

Timothy West..........King Edward VII
Helen Ryan..............Queen Alexandra
Jane Lapotaire...Dowager Empress Dagmar
Christopher Neame......Kaiser Wilhelm II
Moira Redmond.............Alice Keppel
Basil Dignam.................H.H. Asquith
Geoffrey Bayldon.......Sir Henry Campbewll-Bannerman
Michael Osborne..........Prince George
Judy Loe.......................Princess Mary
Edward De Souza......Luis De Soveral
Peter Howell..............Francis Knollys
James Berwick............Sir John Fisher
Basil Hoskins....................Lord Esher
Michael Billington....Czar Nicholas II
Madeleine Cannon.......Princess Toria
Robert Robinson......Sir Ernest Cassel
Denis Lill............Frederick Ponsonby
Geoffrey Beevers....David Lloyd-George
Christopher Strauli......Winston Churchill
Michael Poole.......................Stolypin
Jan Harvey.....Daisy, Princess of Pless

Timothy West

Helen Ryan

Jane Lapotaire

Christopher Neame

Moira Redmond

Basil Dignam

Geoffrey Bayldon

Judy Loe

Barbara Laurenson.......Charlotte Knollys
Sally Home....................Agnes Keyser
Meriel Brooke.......Czarina Alexandra
Helen Dorward.......Empress Augusta
George A. Cooper..Archbishop of Canterbury

Edward De Souza

Peter Howell

Basil Hoskins

Michael Billington

Madeleine Cannon

Robert Robinson

Denis Lill

Geoffrey Beevers

Christopher Strauli

Michael Poole

Jan Harvey

Barbara Laurenson

Sally Home

Meriel Brooke

Helen Dorward

Guy Slater

Laon Maybanke

The King enters his final years in general ill health. He smokes too much and has put on too much weight. But despite this, he continues to work hard for his country.

Britain concludes the triple alliance, concluding a pact with France and Russia but are aware that the German Kaiser, the King's nephew, will inevitably see it as an affront to Germany.

Willie still visits his uncle and appears sincere in his love of family and of England, but his on-going re-armament of the German army and navy is clearly seen as a threat against the United Kingdom.

Basil Dignam, Geoffrey Bayldon

Christopher Strauli, Basil Dignam

Timothy West with the bird

As a counter-balance the King and Queen set off on a trip to Russia to visit his nephew, the Czar. Having to yet again make amends to Willie, the King visits Germany but it takes a serious toll on his health.

In between talks with his nephew the Kaiser, Edward collapses and has a coughing fit. He refuses to have the doctor sent for; he tells Wilhelm they must be seen together. Edward returns to England.

Domestically, the King is thrust into a constitutional cri-
sis when the House of Lords refuses to pass social reforms
passed by the House of Commons. Asquith says a small land
tax may solve many problems.

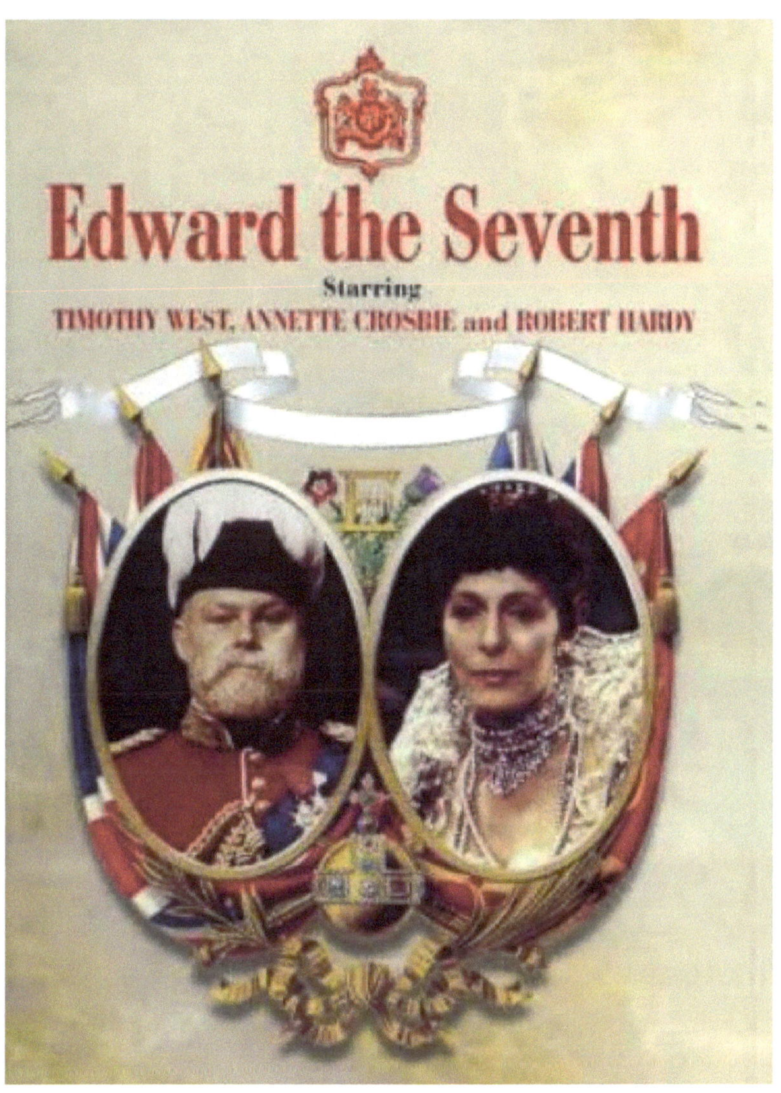

Television Poster

Geoffrey Beevers, Christopher Strauli

Timothy West, Helen Ryan

Edward says that the will of the people should not and cannot be ignored. He implores that a compromise be reached.
Asquith wants a bill cutting down the Lord's power, as well as their right of veto.

108

He says that there is one way to do this-for the King to create hundreds of liberal peers, but Lord Esher says if this is done, it will ruin the prestige and authority of the monarchy.

In Paris, Edward goes to the theatre; on the way back to his hotel, he collapses. His condition worsens from "a chill" to bronchitis. His heart is weakening, and breathing becomes difficult.

Denis Lill, Geoffrey Bayldon

Moira Redmond, Denis Lill

Peter Howell, Basil Hoskins

Christopher Neame, Timothy West

At home, he collapses one more time, and has to be put to bed. Alix realizes he does not have long to live. He dies on May 6, 1910. Prince George informs him that his horse has just won a race. "I am very glad," Edward says, just before taking his last breath.